Tricky Thinking Problen

Advanced activities in applied thi skills for ages 6–11

John Langrehr and Jan Langrehr

Routledge
Taylor & Francis Group

LONDON AND NEW YORK

First published by Curriculum Corporation in Australia in 2002
Reprinted 2003

Published 2008
by Routledge
2 Park Square, Milton Park, Abingdon, Oxon OX14 4RN

Simultaneously published in the USA and Canada
by Routledge
270 Madison Avenue, New York, NY 10016

*Routledge is an imprint of the Taylor & Francis Group, an informa
business*

Printed and bound in Great Britain by Bell & Bain, Ltd., Glasgow

British Library Cataloguing in Publication Data
A catalogue record for this book is available from the British Library

Library of Congress Cataloging-in-Publication Data
Langrehr, John.
  Tricky thinking problems : advanced activities in applied thinking
  skills for ages 6-11 / John Langrehr and Jan Langrehr.
      p. cm.
  ISBN 978–0–415–46591–5 (pbk) – ISBN 978–0–203–92646–8 (ebk)
  1. Thought and thinking – Study and teaching (Elementary)
  2. Critical thinking – Study and teaching (Elementary) 3. Creative
  thinking – Study and teaching (Elementary) I. Langrehr, Jan.
  II. Title.
  LB1590.3.L375 2008
  370.15′2–dc22
  2007048655

ISBN 10: 0-415-46591-5 (pbk)
ISBN 10: 0-203-92646-3 (ebk)
ISBN 13: 978-0-415-46591-5 (pbk)
ISBN 13: 978-0-203-92646-8 (ebk)

Contents

Introduction

The questions in this book test and develop **creative** and **critical thinking**. These are the two most vital forms of thinking for the 21st century. Both kinds of thinking involve pupils asking themselves questions about information. A few questions at the start of each topic also focus on thinking processes that help pupils mentally organise information better.

The 20 or more basic thinking processes that pupils need in our rapidly changing and information-rich world are shown at the end of this introduction. The questions in the book are designed to test and develop most of them. Classroom questions have traditionally focused on testing the recall, understanding, and application of content and methods. These do little for helping pupils to think flexibly about possibilities and to make independent judgements about information, when they leave school.

Hence the need for constant practice questions that demand these higher forms of thinking, if an individual is to reach his or her intellectual potential.

Who is this book for?

This is a book for pupils in upper primary school and early secondary school. Younger pupils will not have the content knowledge needed in the exercises. **Average pupils** will find the exercises useful and interesting. **Gifted pupils** however also find the questions challenging because many invite a range of answers that gifted students can readily provide. **ESL pupils** will also find many questions useful, especially those that test processes such as comparing, categorising, ordering, and generalising.

How can you check the answers?

Suggested answers are given at the end of the book. Because the questions test and develop analytical, creative, and critical thinking, as well as understanding, a variety of answers are possible. In general, the answers at the back of the book are a good guide. If pupils have other answers, they should check them with other pupils or adults to see if they are acceptable!

Do you need to do more than check answers?

Good thinking doesn't happen simply by getting correct answers to someone else's questions. Good thinking develops by learning to ask yourself good questions. If a pupil doesn't know how to answer a particular question, it is important for a teacher, parent, or older pupil to talk aloud about the questions they asked themselves in answering the question. This sharing of the thought processes of good thinkers is the most powerful way of learning to think better. A guide to these thinking processes is offered in the following section.

John and Jan Langrehr

Thinking Processes

Listed below are the common thinking processes tested and developed by the questions in this book.

For MENTALLY ORGANISING information in the brain

- Observing similarities
- Observing differences
- Categorising similar things into groups
- Ordering things in terms of their size
- Ordering things in order of time
- Generalising about given examples
- Analysing parts and relationships
- Visual summarising
- Designing your own questions
- Predicting

For THINKING CRITICALLY about information

- Identifying facts, non-facts, opinions
- Identifying definite from indefinite conclusions
- Identifying assumptions
- Judging the reliability of claims
- Judging relevant from irrelevant information
- Making decisions
- Identifying causes and effects
- Considering other points of view

For THINKING CREATIVELY about information

- Reverse creative thinking
- Analysing the creativity of designs
- Creative consequences
- Creative comparisons
- Creative uses
- Creative random ideas
- Creative combinations

Useful Questions

Here are a few comments about the thinking processes tested in the exercises. There are also some useful questions for pupils to ask themselves when using these processes.

When looking for similarities and differences

Our brains are like mental filing cabinets. They like to store things we observe in an organised way, according to the various properties they have. For example, we have a 'mental folder' for red things, round things, living things, animals, wild animals, large-wild animals, and so on. The thinking process of comparing involves us looking for **similarities** and **differences** in the things we observe. Some useful properties to compare in things are their size, colour, use, material, parts, and shape . . . t he first letters of these properties spell the word **SCUMPS**!

Encourage pupils to ask themselves this question when comparing:
*Do these things have the same or different **shape**, **colour**, **use**, **material**, **parts**, **size**?*
Eg. What are two ways in which a cow and a horse are the same/different?

When looking to group or categorise

Our brain organises things that have the **same property** into a **category** or **group**. Your category labeled 'round things' might include tyres, coins, oranges, records, and so on. Examples of these different things will all be stored in the category of 'round things' in our brains. If you are asked to name some round things, these examples come forward very quickly out of your memory.

Encourage pupils to ask themselves this question when categorising:
Do these two or more things have the same size, colour, use, material, parts, shape or other features in common?
Eg. How are all of these things similar? A horse, an ant, a fish.
     Which one of these is different and why? A horse, an ant, a fish.

When looking to put things into an order

Our brains are very clever in not only organising examples of something in terms of their common properties, but also in terms of their **order** in a particular property. For example, animals are placed in order of their size, geometric figures in order of their number of sides, metals in order of their hardness or expense, or methods of transport in order of their speed.

Encourage pupils to ask themselves these questions when ordering:
What property do all of these things have in common?
Which thing has the smallest amount of this property? This will be first in the order.
Which has the most amount of this property? This will be last in the order.
Eg. Place these things in an order and say what property you used to place them in this order…a mouse, a bird, a whale

When making a generalisation from given examples

Our brains store for us all the different properties that examples of something usually have. For example, your brain may have remembered for you that sports often have a referee, a ball, a bat, rules, a winner, a field, and so on. But do *all* sports have all of these properties? No! Some sports don't need a referee or a ball or a bat. But there are some properties that are common to all sports. These form a **generalisation** or mental picture we have of something that contains **all of the properties common to all examples of this thing**.

Encourage pupils to ask themselves these questions when generalising:
Can I picture in my mind five or more examples of this thing?
What are some parts or features of these examples?
Can I list them?
Which parts/features are common to all examples on my list?
Eg. What properties do all examples of flowers have in common?

When wondering why a thing has a particular design or feature

This thinking process helps us to become more sensitive to the creativity about us. Everything made by humans or nature has a **design** that fits a **special function** of that thing. Coins don't just happen to be round for fun. Trees don't just happen to have a round trunk and thousands of leaves for no good reason. These features of their design serve a particular function. When we ask ourselves the question 'Why does this thing have this size, colour, shape, material . . . rather than some other possibility?' we are asking the same question that the original creator of the thing asked him or herself.

Being sensitive to the creativity about us is one of the first steps in developing our own creative thought processes.

Encourage pupils to ask themselves these questions when thinking creatively about designs:
Why does this creation/design have this . . .
Shape rather than other shapes?
Colour rather than other colours?
Use rather than other uses?
Material rather than other materials?
Part(s) rather than other parts?
Size rather than other sizes?
Eg. What are three reasons for bottles being made of glass?

When deciding if a statement is fact or opinion

Statements we read or hear can either be a fact, an opinion, or untrue. Not everything we read in a newspaper, or hear on TV, is a fact. Unfortunately, many people have never been taught how to distinguish a **fact** from an **opinion**. This thinking process is one of the many related to what is called critical thinking or judgmental thinking. Here are some useful questions that good critical thinkers report they ask themselves when trying to decide what is a fact and what is an opinion.

Encourage pupils to ask themselves these questions when distinguishing statements that are facts from statements that are opinions. If the answer to any of these questions is '**yes**', then the statement is a **fact**. If the answer is '**no**', then the statement is an **opinion**.
Can this statement be proven scientifically or with evidence?
Has this event already happened in the past?
Does this statement contain definite words like is, was, has, . . . ?
Does this statement contain definite numerical measurements?
Was this statement made by a reputable authority?
Eg. Men are better pilots than women. Fact or opinion?

'Yes' = Fact
'No' = Opinion

When judging the reliability of a claim

We often see on TV or read in the newspaper about someone who claims to have seen a UFO, a monster, an extinct animal, and so on. How do you know whether to believe him or her? Is the 'witness' or the newspaper **reliable**? This is another critical thinking skill because it involves making judgements about statements.

7

Encourage pupils to ask themselves these questions when judging the reliability of a claim made:

Did he/she see it first hand?
Did anyone else see it?
Does she/he have any vested interests in this?
How close was he/she to the scene?
Was he/she in sound mind at the time?
Is he/she well respected by colleagues?
Has he/she sought publicity about this issue before?
How experienced is he/she? . . . .

Eg. In this statement made by Mr X in the newspaper what are three statements made that help us to believe that his claim is true.

When trying to distinguish between a definite and an uncertain conclusion about a picture or advertisement

Advertisers often try to get people to make a conclusion about an advertisement or picture when there is simply no evidence for the conclusion they make. People are quick to make inferences or draw conclusions about things they read and see. They love to 'read between the lines'. But you can only make **definite conclusions** about things you can **directly observe**. This critical thinking skill is easy if you get students to ask themselves questions like those that follow.

Encourage students to ask themselves these questions when deciding whether they can make a definite or an unsure conclusion about things they read or see.

Is there observable evidence here to prove my conclusion? . . . D efinite
Is my conclusion about feelings and beliefs that I can't see? . . . U nsure
Is my conclusion about things that I can't see? . . . U nsure
Is my conclusion about things that will happen in the future? . . . U nsure
Am I making assumptions (reading between the lines) here without evidence?
Do I have any evidence to support this conclusion I make? . . .

Eg. Underline the words in this paper advertisement that you can't be sure of. In other words, different people might interpret the meaning of the words differently.

'All bikes will be sold at a big discount this week.'

When distinguishing causes from effects

Causes and their effects are directly related to each other. An effect follows a cause and results from it.

Critical thinkers can easily judge whether an event is a cause or an effect by asking themselves a simple question like the one here.

Which event here follows after (the effect), and is directly related to, another event (the cause)?

Eg. Underline the cause and circle the effect in this sentence:
The boys did not go sailing today because the wind was too strong.

When judging if a picture or reading is biased

Critical thinkers are quick to judge whether a picture, story, or advertisement is **biased** or **prejudiced** against a particular group of people. Such things can be negatively biased against the old, weak, poor, females or foreigners. Critical thinkers are fair minded. That is they are prepared to consider things from the **opposite** viewpoint to their own.

8

Encourage pupils to ask themselves this question when trying to judge whether a statement, story, picture, or advertisement is biased or not.
Is this group of people shown in an unflattering light (lazy, non-professional, frightened, needing help, unintelligent, poor, old or sick)?

When deciding if something is relevant/irrelevant
When making a decision, we try to think of some **important or relevant factors** to consider that will help us make our decision. How do we know what is relevant?

Here are some useful questions to ask yourself for this critical thinking skill.
What is the main goal or purpose here?
Which of these features are really important /useful in achieving this goal?
Will this feature or property really help me achieve my goal?(irrelevant if no)
Eg. What are three relevant properties to consider when buying a pet dog?
       What are two irrelevant factors to consider?

When analysing parts and their relationships
This thinking process or skill is related to analytical thinking. It is easy if you ask yourself the following questions.
How is the second thing in the pair related to the first?
What does the fourth thing have to be so it has this same relationship with the third thing?
Eg. Eagle is to bird as salmon is to . . .

Suggested Question Use

1. Photocopy the content summary passage for each topic (Animals, Insects, etc), together with the set of questions. Allow pupils ample time to complete the questions. You may of course choose to select some questions for pupils to attempt individually, and others for discussion as a class.

2. Call for answers to a question. More than one answer is possible for most questions. Allow pupils to justify their answers if they are unusual.

3. Ask a successful pupil to talk aloud about the questions that passed through his or her mind in coming up with the answer. These questions may include the patterns observed, the key words in a sentence, the mental pictures used, a personal strategy, and so on. This process of reflection and talking aloud is called **metacognition**. It is the most powerful method for improving the thinking and learning of a pupil. Just hearing good answers to a question does not achieve this.

4. Talk about the type of thinking process involved in each question. Share the information in the summary of these processes that follows these notes. For example, if the question involves the distinguishing of facts from opinions, share the kind of questions that good critical thinkers ask themselves when using this thinking process. In this way, all pupils are improving their content intelligence and also their processing intelligence. That is, they are improving the range of questions they can ask themselves when thinking in a particular way in future.

Animals

Living things are either plants or animals. Most animals move around and feed on other animals or plants. Most plants are fixed to the ground and make their own food.

About one million different kinds of animals have been found by scientists. Hundreds of new ones are found each year. Some one-celled animals are so small that they can only he seen under a microscope.

When we think of animals, we mainly think of animals classified as vertebrates. These are animals that have a rod-like structure (spine and skeleton) in their backs to support their bodies. There are many different groups of vertebrates – reptiles, birds, fishes, amphibians and mammals.

We can also group animals in other ways. For example, animals can be warm or cold blooded, water or land living, tame or wild, have two legs, four legs and so on. Humans have two legs, while snakes have none.

Some animals eat plants. However, many animals eat each other for food. In this way, the number of animals is kept under control. This is called ecological balance, or sometimes the 'Web of Life'.

For years, humans have killed many different kinds of wild animals for sport or those that are useful for food. However, today we realise that we need to protect some animals, otherwise they will no longer exist on the Earth.

Dogs were probably the first animals tamed by humans. They shared the meat killed by humans and helped them to hunt other animals. Eventually humans also tamed other animals that they liked to eat.

Most of the large animals that are harmful to humans have been reduced in numbers, or are confined to remote areas such as jungles or deserts. Some very tiny animals, such as bacteria and mosquitoes, are still dangerous to us because it is hard to see them and because they exist in such large numbers.

Animals protect themselves in different ways. Some run very quickly, while others have sharp claws, teeth, spikes and beaks or hard shells and horns. Others use poisonous liquids and stings. Some hide in small holes, fly in the air, or use camouflage.

Mammals (of which we are a species) are vertebrates. They tend to have a large brain. They feed their young on mother's milk and protect them carefully. The largest mammal is the 30 metre long blue whale. The most intelligent living animal is our own species, *homo sapiens* (human beings).

Animals

1. Three of these animals are **different** from the other three in some way. Circle them and say why they are different.

rabbit   lion   cow   horse   shark   dog

They are different because . . . .

_____

_____

_____

2. The following animals have been placed in **order**. Which property common to all of them was used to place them in this order?

birds   dogs   humans

Property used _____

3. Ben found a dead bird in his driveway. He concluded that it must have been killed by a cat. What is he **assuming** (what else may have killed the bird)? What **evidence** would he need to help prove his conclusion?

_____

_____

_____

_____

4. Name three ways in which a **cat** is **different** from a **dog**.

_____

_____

_____

5. Why do you think a cat has four legs rather than two?

_____

_____

_____

6. Snakes, birds, frogs, humans, and fish are all animals. List as many parts of these different animals as possible.

_____

_____

_____

Now cross off the ones that are NOT COMMON to ALL of these animals. What **generalisation** can you make about animals?

Generalisation... All animals have

_____

_____

_____

7. Complete the following so that the last two things are **related** in the same way as the first two things.

Rose is to flower   as   eagle is to _____

Sparrow is to fly   as   shark is to _____

Snake is to hiss   as   dog is to _____

8. Complete the following by placing words in the blanks.

If there were no more birds in the world then_____

_____and this would mean that

_____.

9. Write down a reason **for**, and a reason **against**, allowing hunters to kill great white sharks.

For

_____

_____

Against

_____

_____

10. Can you think of three things that cats can **never** do?

_____

_____

_____

11. Write down three ways in which a crab is the **same as** a fish.

_____

_____

Now write down three ways in which it is **different from** a fish.

_____

_____

_____

12. How could you **weigh a horse**?

_____

_____

_____

13. List five **relevant factors** to consider in choosing a pet.

_____

_____

_____

Now list three **irrelevant factors** to consider.

_____

_____

_____

14. If someone **claimed** to have seen an extinct Tasmanian Tiger what are three questions you would like answered before believing the person?

_____

_____

_____

Insects

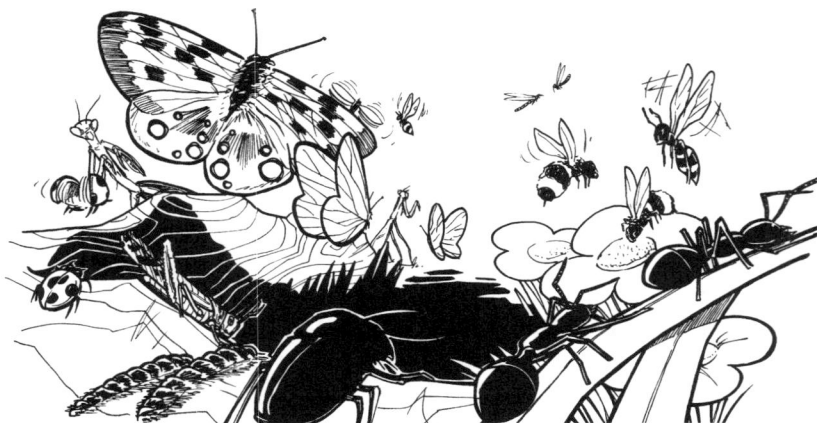

Insects are small, six-legged animals. All kinds of flies, moths, bees, ants, bugs and beetles are insects. Spiders, which have eight legs, are in a different category (arachnids). Scientists have identified about one million different insects on Earth.

Fossils over 400 hundred million years old contain outlines of insects. Insects have obviously survived the toughest of conditions. They can eat almost anything and can live in even freezing and cramped places. Another reason that insects have lived so long is their ability to lay hundreds of eggs early in their life.

Insects have distinct three section bodies: head, thorax (middle) and abdomen. They have two antennae on their head through which they smell. They hear through hairs or holes on their bodies. Because insects don't have noses or lungs, they breathe through the holes on their bodies. Most insects have wings, which are often protected under a hard shell. Their wings help them to find food and escape from enemies.

Insects protect themselves from enemies by the use of sprays, stings and colours (which blend in with their surroundings).

Insects have their own blood system to live. However, they don't have veins and arteries like us. Their cold, yellowish blood simply fills their body and surrounds their organs. The brain of an insect receives messages from the antennae, ears and eyes. Their eyes, which are always open, have many lenses, which can see things for a distance of only about one metre. The ears of insects are placed all over their bodies or legs. Some insects hear the sounds made by other insects through the hairs on their antennae.

Some people think of insects as a nuisance, but they are in fact very useful. Bees and other insects help humans by pollinating fruit trees, vegetables, flowers crops. Bees also produce honey and wax that we use. Many insects feed on rotting plants and creatures, breaking them down and destroying the toxins in them. Birds, fish and reptiles often feed on insects. Humans, in turn, then eat these fish and birds. This is called a 'food chain'.

Some insects are a threat to us. Flies, cockroaches, beetles and termites help decompose material, but they can also carry diseases and destroy timber and other materials. We can control large numbers of harmful insects by using chemicals called insecticides, or we can use other helpful insects that feed on them. Ladybirds are an example of insects that eat other pest insects (aphids) which are a threat to plants.

The life cycle of insects such as flies and butterflies is interesting. The adult fly lays eggs, which hatch to form maggots or larvae. These maggots harden to form pupae, from which, after an interval, emerge adult flies – which in turn keep the life cycle going.

Many insects make life difficult for us. And yet without certain insects, life as we know it would cease.

Insects

1. Write down three ways in which a **butterfly** is **different** from a **bird**.

_____

_____

_____

2. Underline the two **facts** here.

a. Insects are not as useful to humans as birds.

b. Insects always have 6 legs.

c. Insects have existed on the Earth for millions of years.

d. The number of insects in the world will increase in future.

Why are they facts?

_____

_____

3. Write down some **properties** or features of these insects.

flies   bees   moths   ladybirds

Share your answers to create a big list.

Properties

_____

_____

_____

Now cross out those properties that are **not common** to **all** of your insects? Your **generalisation** about insects should only contain those properties that are common to all insects.

4. Why do you think a bee:

a. has **6 legs** rather than 4?

_____

_____

b. has **black and yellow stripes**?

_____

_____

5. Complete the following:

a. Bee is to insect   as   apple is to _____

b. Ant is to six   as   spider is to _____

c. Human is to nose   as   insect is to _____

6. Complete the following by placing **words** in the **blanks**.

If there were no more bees in the world then _____

_____and this would mean that_____

_____ .

7. Write down **one reason for**, and **one reason against**, corn farmers spraying their crops with insecticides.

For

_____

_____

Against

_____

_____

8. Would you believe that a **cricket** and a **TV set** are the **same** in many ways? Can you write down three or more of them?

_____

_____

_____

9. Can you think of three places where you **wouldn't** find a **fly**?

_____

_____

10. Three of the following insects are **different** from the other three. Circle them. Say why they are different.

    bees   mosquitoes   fleas   butterflies   lady birds   cockroaches

They are different because

_____

_____

11. Fill in the missing stages, and connectors in the life cycle map here.

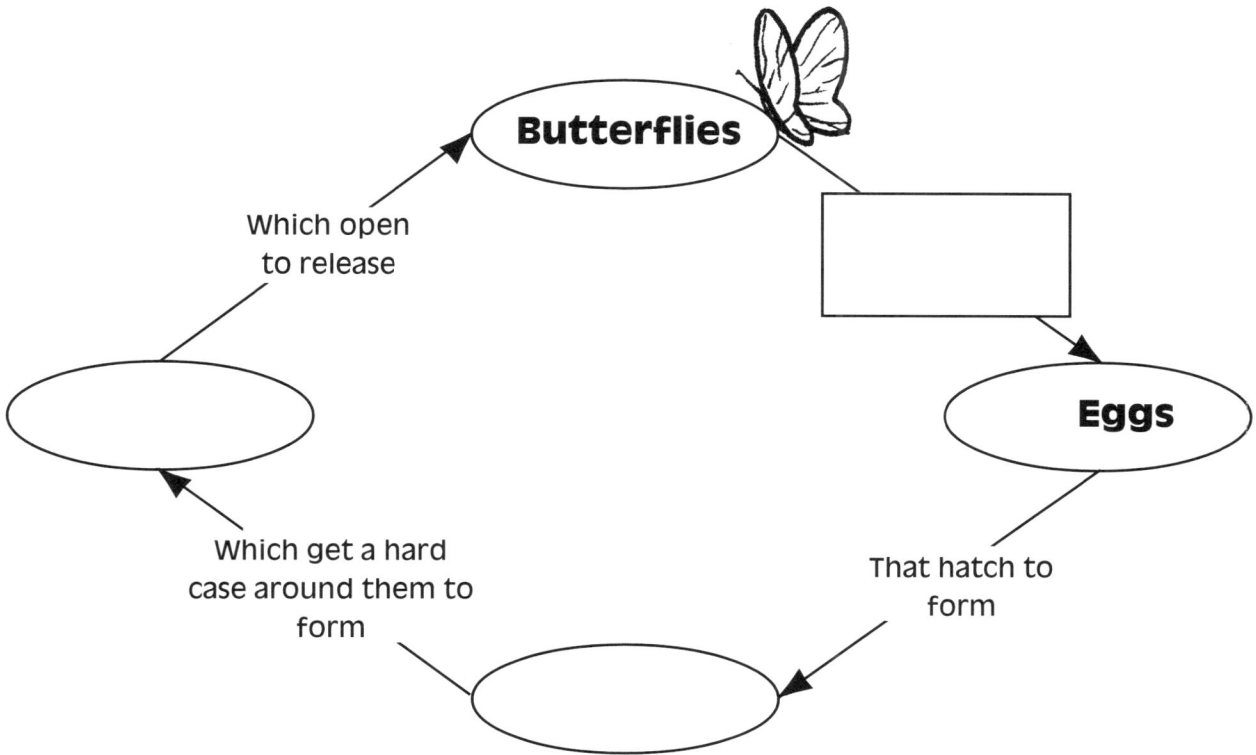

Butterflies

Which open
to release

[ ]

Eggs

Which get a hard
case around them to
form

That hatch to
form

Plants

Plants are living things that are usually fixed to the ground. Without plants there could be no life! Plants make oxygen for us to breathe. Much of our food, shelter and clothing also comes from plants.

Scientists have found over 300,000 different kinds of plants.

Like animals, the smallest plants can be seen only with a microscope. The largest plants are sequoia trees, which can reach 88 metres in height and 9 metres in width.

The cells of plants are different from animal cells. Plant cells have thick walls made of cellulose.

Scientists have placed the different plants into groups.

Algae and fungi don't have roots, stems or leaves. Mosses, ferns, pines, flowers, shrubs and trees in general have these parts and reproduce using male and female sex organs.

Most plants have roots, stems (or trunks), leaves and flowers. Roots hold the plant firmly in the ground and take up water and chemicals from the soil. Stems hold the leaves and flowers and lift them up so that they can receive plenty of sunlight.

Leaves are the food factory of the plant. Their green chemical, called chlorophyll, unites the water (from the ground), carbon dioxide (from the air) and light (from the sun) to form starch. Starch makes the stems of plants grow.

Flowers are the reproductive parts of plants. They contain the male stamens and the female pistils. Pollen grains from a stamen fertilise the egg in a pistil to form a seed.

The roots and leaves of many plants provide us with food. Trees also provide us with wood, coal, fruits, cotton, paper, nuts and chemicals.

Plants and animals form a life cycle. Plants make oxygen, which is breathed in by humans and other animals. The animals breathe out carbon dioxide, which is taken in by plants so that they can make their own food. Plants also use water and chemicals from the soil and light energy from the sun to make food. Chemicals are returned to the soil when animals and plants die.

Different kinds of plants grow in different regions of the Earth. The plants on high mountains differ from those in tropical forests, deserts, swamps, coastlines and the sea.

Humans have killed many types of plants, but now we are trying to conserve those plants which have very few examples left on the Earth, particularly the plants of rainforests.

Plants

1. Write down three ways in which a **plant** is the **same as** an **animal**.

_____

_____

_____

Now write down three ways in which a **plant** is **different** from an **animal**.

_____

_____

_____

2. The following things have been placed in an **order**. What **property** of them was used to place them in this order?

        roots   trunk   branches   twigs   leaves

Property used _____

3. Write down two **relevant** or **important** things to consider about a tree when choosing one to plant in your yard.

_____

_____

_____

Now write down two **irrelevant** or **unimportant** things to consider.

_____

_____

_____

4. Two of the following statements are **facts**. The other is an **opinion**. Underline the **opinion**.

a. Roses are the prettiest of all the flowers.

b. Roses usually have thorns.

c. Roses exist in many different colours.

Why is it an opinion?

_____

_____

_____

19

5. In the morning Mrs Gardener found that some of the apples on her apple tree had fallen on the ground. What are two things she can **definitely be sure of**? What are two things she **can't be sure of** without proof?

Sure of

_____

_____

Can't be sure of

_____

_____

6. Write down at least three **properties** that all of these examples of trees have in **common**. You can use four other trees that you know if you prefer.

an oak tree   a fig tree   a gum tree   an apple tree

_____

_____

_____

Can you name any trees that **don't have** any of these properties?

_____

_____

7. Why do you think a tree has **thousands of leaves** rather than ten or twenty?

_____

_____

_____

8. Complete the following so that the last two things are related in the same way as the first two things.

Plant is to sap   as   animal is to _____

Plant is to carbon dioxide   as   animal is to _____

9. Complete the following by placing words in the blanks.

If there were no more trees in the world then _____

_____ and this would mean that_____

_____ .

10. Write down **one reason for**, and **one reason against**, people in some countries cutting down thousands of trees from their rain forests.

For

_____

Against

_____

11. Would you believe that a **tree** and a **car** are the **same** in many ways? Can you write down three or more of them?

_____

_____

_____

12. Name three places where you **wouldn't** find flowers growing.

_____

_____

_____

13. Write in the missing **cause** or **effect** in the following table.

Cause	Effect
	branches snapped off trees
	fruit ripens on trees
sap stops flowing in trees	
nectar on flowers of plants	

14. The answer is **Trees**. Write down three questions with this answer.

_____

_____

_____

21

Whales

Whales are not fish. Fish have gills for breathing in air that is dissolved in water. On the other hand, whales use lungs to breath in air from above the ocean in which they live.

What's more, whales are mammals, just like cats, horses and humans. This means that whales have warm blood and give milk to their young.

Blue whales grow up to 30 metres in length. They are one of the largest of all animals, although there are some fully grown whales, called pygmy whales, which measure only a few metres long.

Some whales can stay under water for over one hour before coming up to the surface to breathe the air. This is amazing when you consider that the world record for human beings is a mere 6 minutes!

Whales have a reasonably sized brain, which makes them among the most intelligent of all animals. Scientists have recorded noises that whales use to 'talk' to each other.

Unlike sharks, most whales don't have a very good sense of smell. They also don't have very good eyesight or sense of taste. All whales have very large mouths. Some have quite small teeth, while others don't have any teeth at all.

During the summer months, whales migrate or swim thousands of kilometres to the cold oceans of the North and South Poles. When winter comes, they migrate back towards the equator, where the water is much warmer.

Mother whales generally have only one calf at a time. Whales live for between fifteen and forty years.

Humans are the main enemies of whales. Fishermen from some countries still try to kill them for meat. Whale oil is also used to make soap, lamp oil, and various chemicals. Because of uncontrolled hunting, some species came close to extinction (the blue whale, shown above, dropping to less than 1000 world-wide). Nowadays however, whales are protected, as the world attempts to preserve these unique creatures.

Whales

1. Write down three ways in which a **whale** is the **same** as a **shark**.

_____

_____

_____

Now write three ways in which it is **different** from a shark.

_____

_____

_____

2. Three of these animals are **different from** the other three in some way. Circle them and say why they are different.

whales   cows   snakes   lizards   dogs   fish

Different because _____

_____

_____

3. Write down two **facts** about whales.

_____

_____

_____

Now write down two **opinions** about whales.

_____

_____

_____

4. Why do you think a whale has such a **large mouth**?

_____

_____

_____

Why don't whales generally have **sharp teeth**?

_____

_____

_____

5. Complete the following:

a. Whale is to calf   as   fowl is to _____

b. Whale is to mammal   as   snake is to _____

c. Blubber is to whale   as   _____ is to human.

6. Complete the following by placing **words** in the **blanks**.

If there were no more whales in the world then _____

_____ and this would mean that _____

_____ .

7. Write down **one reason for** and **one reason against** some people killing whales with harpoons.

For

_____

_____

_____

Against

_____

_____

_____

8. Would you believe that a **whale** and a **car** are the **same** in many ways? Can you write down three or more of them?

_____

_____

_____

9. Write down three or more questions you would like to have answered before possibly believing a boy who claimed to have seen a **white whale** while fishing from the jetty.

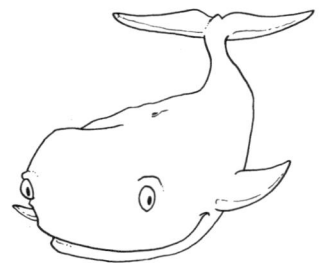

_____

_____

_____

_____

10. Make up two questions about **whales** starting with a word from Row A and then one from Row B. Answer your questions.

Row A	What	Where	When	Which	Who	Why	How
Row B	Is	Did	Can	Would	Will	Might	

eg Q. Who might want to kill whales?
   A. People who use chemicals from them to make perfume.

Question 1

_____

_____

Answer

_____

Question 2

_____

_____

Answer

_____

Weather

The temperature, movement, pressure and moisture content of the air around us changes from day to day. Experts forecast these changes for us because the weather on a particular day really affects what we wear and do.

Extremes in the weather can affect such things as crops, movement on roads, sales of particular goods, the travel industry, transport schedules, and so on. Weather is what happens on a particular day. Climate is different: it's the *average* weather for a region over many years.

Weather Forecasting

This is difficult to do because the weather changes quickly. However, it is important, especially for warning boats and aeroplanes of approaching dangers. Forecasters collect data from weather monitoring stations, as well as the captains of aeroplanes and ships. Forecasters summarise these data and display them as daily weather maps.

Weather Maps

These maps show fronts, wind, rain, air pressure and temperature. A front is a curved line that involves a big difference in the weather. The air pressure is marked on the many curved lines on a weather map. High pressure means fine weather; low pressure usually means wind and cloudy weather. The closer the pressure lines on a map, the windier the weather, because there are large changes in air pressure. The strength and direction of the wind is shown by arrows with different types of tails.

The temperature of our atmosphere is dependent on the energy given off by the Sun. The clouds and air trap this energy when it hits the Earth so that we keep warm. The closer a region of the Earth is to the Sun (for example, at or near the Equator) the warmer it is.

Wind is moving air. The greater the difference of the air pressure between places, the stronger the movement of air, or wind – always from high to low pressure. In a tornado, the wind can move at up to 480 kilometres per hour.

The air contains moisture (or water) due to evaporation. In suspension, it is fog or humidity. When heavy enough, it falls to the Earth as rain, hail or snow.

Air pressure is measured with a barometer. A sudden change in air pressure usually indicates a change in the weather. Scientists use weather satellites to study the movement of clouds around the Earth's surface. These help to forecast rain and violent storms much more accurately.

Weather

1. Write down three ways in which **clouds** are the **same** as **lakes**.

_____

_____

_____

Now write in three ways in which clouds are **different** from lakes.

_____

_____

_____

2. Place the following things in an **order**. What **property** of them did you use to place them in this order?

rain   lightning   flood   thunder

My order _____

Reason for my order _____

_____

3. Three of the following are **different** from the other three. Circle them and say why they are different.

rain   breeze   tornado   snow   wind   fog

Different because

_____

_____

_____

4. Underline the **fact** here.

a. Snow is prettier to watch than rain.

b. Rain is made of the same thing as snow.

c. Snow is more dangerous to drivers than rain.

d. Air pressure is measured with a thermometer.

Why is it a fact?

_____

_____

_____

5. Write in the missing **causes** or **effects**.

Cause	Effect
	a rainbow
	thunder
no rain	

6. List some **disadvantages** of an **umbrella**.

_____

_____

_____

What **changes** would you make to the design to **remove** these **disadvantages**?

_____

_____

_____

7. Can you think of three places where you **wouldn't** find air?

_____

_____

_____

8. Complete the following.

a. Water is to rain   as   _____ is to wind.

b. Rain is to flood   as   lightning is to _____ .

C. Thermometer is to temperature   as   _____ is to pressure.

9. Complete the following by placing **words** in the **blanks**.

If we no longer had weather forecasts then _____

_____ and this would mean that _____

_____ .

10. Write in the missing words on this summary map about air.

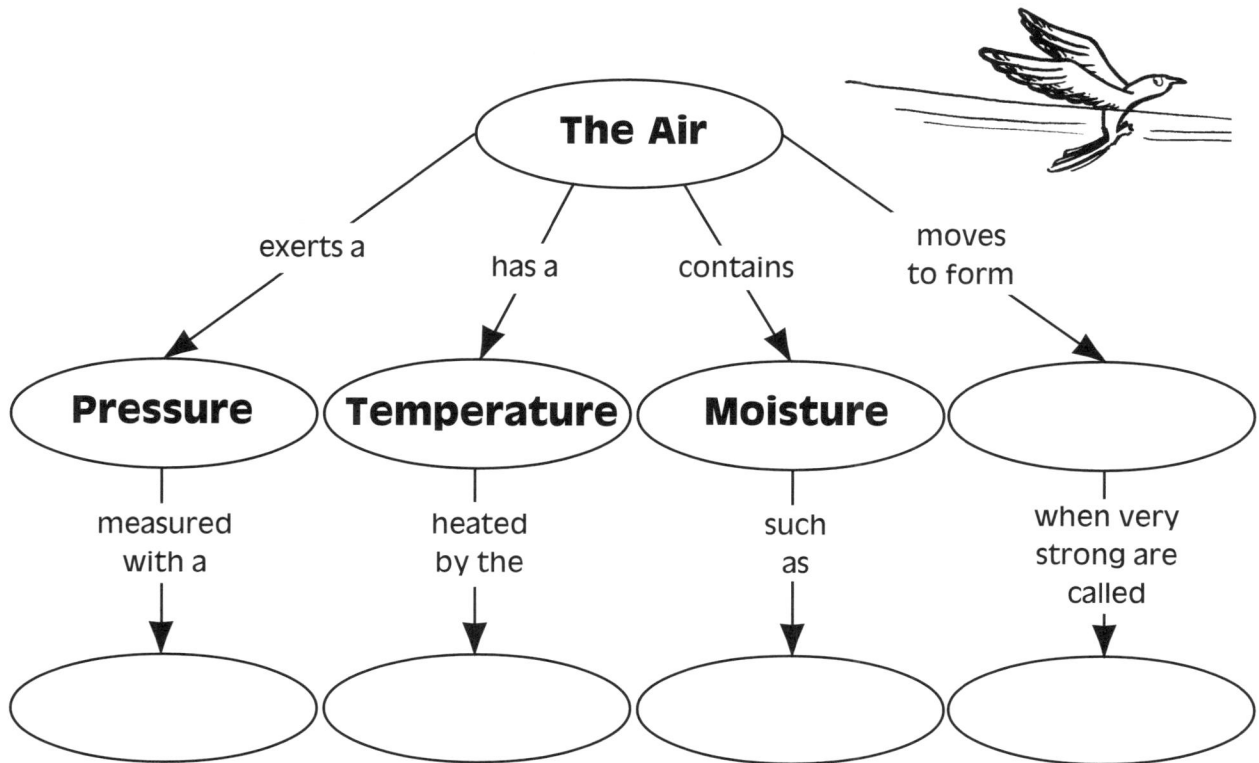

```
                         The Air
        exerts a      has a    contains    moves
                                           to form

     Pressure    Temperature    Moisture    (        )

   measured       heated         such       when very
   with a         by the         as         strong are
                                            called

   (      )       (      )       (     )     (        )
```

TRICKY THINKING PROBLEMS

Planets

The Earth is one of nine planets that make up our solar system – rotating around the heart of the system – our Sun. The Sun is a star or hot ball of gas that produces its *own* heat and light.

The planet Mercury is closest to the Sun, followed by Venus, Earth, Mars, Jupiter, Saturn, Uranus, Neptune and Pluto. Jupiter is the largest planet, Mercury the smallest, and Pluto the second smallest.

It takes the Earth, the fifth largest planet, one year (or 365.1 days) to travel around the Sun. Planets close to the Sun are hot and others far away from the Sun are cold. None give off light, but we can see them because they all *reflect* light from the Sun.

Moons

The Earth is one planet that has a moon. This is a satellite (or mini-planet) which circles round a planet. The moon takes one month to pass around the Earth. Of the nine planets, only Mercury, Venus and Pluto *don't* have moons.

Atmospheres

The Earth is the only planet with a large amount of oxygen in its atmosphere. Other planets have gases such as hydrogen and ammonia around them.

The average temperature on the surface of the Earth is 14 degrees Celsius. The two planets closest to the *Sun* have temperatures of more than 200 degrees Celsius, while those further from the Sun than the Earth have temperatures of about minus 60 to minus 180 degrees Celsius.

In 1543, a scientist called Copernicus suggested that the planets, including the Earth, travelled around the Sun. Religious leaders called him a fool and would not allow him to talk about his ideas, because until then people believed that the Sun travelled around the Earth.

Some facts about the four planets closest to the Sun

	Mercury	Venus	Earth	Mars
Diameter (miles)	3100	7600	8000	4200
Number of moons	0	0	1	2
Days to go around Sun	88	225	365	687
Temperature (degrees C)	175	425	15	-25

Planets

1. Write down three ways in which the **Earth** is the **same** as the **moon**.

_____

_____

_____

Now write in three ways in which the Earth is **different** from the moon.

_____

_____

_____

2. The following things have been placed in an **order**. What **property** of them was used to place them in this order?

Mercury   Earth   Mars   Saturn

Property used _____

3. Underline the one **fact** here.

a. There are more planets like Earth in outer space.

b. Mercury is an older planet than the Earth.

c. There are no living creatures on the moon.

d. Eventually, humans will not be able to live on the Earth.

Why is it a fact?

_____

_____

_____

4. Why do you think planets are **round** in shape?

_____

_____

_____

5. Complete the following.

Earth is to planet   as   Sun is to _____

6. Use a textbook or notes to write in **yes** or **no** for the **properties** of planets on the table below.

Then write down those properties that are common to all planets.

	Has moons	Has oxygen	Is a solid	Spins on own axis	Spins around the sun
Earth					
Saturn					
Uranus					
Venus					

My generalisation is . . .

All planets _____

_____

_____

7. Complete the following by placing **words** in the **blanks**.

If the Earth no longer had a moon then _____

_____ and this would mean that _____

_____.

8. The answer is **Sun**. Create three questions with this answer.

_____

_____

_____

9. An astronomer claims to have observed a comet in such a path that it will hit the Earth in less than 5 years time. List at least **five questions** you would like answered before you become concerned that he is right.

_____

_____

_____

_____

TRICKY THINKING PROBLEMS

10. The first five planets from the Sun are Mercury, Venus, Earth, Mars, and Jupiter. From the table of information provided about the first four planets what do you predict about the:

a. number of days it takes Jupiter to circle the Sun?

_____

_____

b. temperature on the surface of Jupiter?

_____

_____

c. number of moons Jupiter has?

_____

_____

Use a reference book to check your predictions.

11. One of the following in each group is **different** in some way to the other three. Circle it. Say why it is different.

Group	Why different
Mercury Moon Venus Mars	
Pluto Venus Sun Mars	
Earth Venus Mars Mercury	

Birds

Birds are feathered vertebrates. Although their wings are what makes them distinctive, not all birds can fly. The world's largest bird, the African Ostrich (weighing up to 150kg and standing 2 metres tall), is unable to fly.

Wings are remarkable structures. The bones are light but strong. The feathers are flexible and can be curved to control wind flow. Some birds have enormous wings which they beat slowly. The albatross has a wing span up to 3 metres long. Other birds have tiny wings which they beat very fast. The hummingbird beats its wings up to 90 times per second!

Depending on size and species, birds eat a variety of foods – hunting other animals or catching insects, or living on seeds and fruit.

Birds use calls for mating, and to tell each other where they are. The calls also warn of enemies nearby.

All birds lay eggs, curved incubating capsules for the young chicks. Most birds lay only ten to twenty eggs each year. However, domestic hens can lay three hundred or more eggs each year.

Before birds hatch from their eggs, the eggs have to be kept warm. This takes from two to eight weeks, depending on the size of the eggs.

Birds are warm blooded, like humans. In summer time they often wash themselves in pools of water to keep cool. In winter, some types of birds fly to the other side of the world. They migrate like this to have their babies in a warm climate.

Birds	Have a nest	Lay eggs	Have feathers	Can fly	Eat seeds
Eagle	yes	yes	yes	yes	no
Magpie	yes	yes	yes	yes	no
Emu	yes	yes	yes	no	yes
Penguin	yes	yes	yes	no	no

Birds

1. Write down a **generalisation** (general statement) that applies to all birds.

_____

_____

_____

2. Complete the following lines, making a sensible **sentence** about each topic.

Topic	Sentence
eg. Birds	lay eggs in a nest.
Eggs	
Wings	
Feathers	

3. Now ask **why** or **how** of each sentence you have made. Write down your questions and try to **answer** them.

Eg. Why do birds lay eggs in a nest? To keep them warm and away from enemies.

Topic 1 _____

_____

Topic 2 _____

_____

Topic 3 _____

_____

4. The following things have been placed in an **order**. What **property** of them was used to place them in this order?

leaves   caterpillar   bird   cat

Property used _____

5. Chang writes a lost bird notice to place in shop windows near his home. Underline the parts that you think are **useful** or **relevant** in helping someone find his bird.

My bird is called Tommy. I bought it last year. It cost me 10 pounds. It has black feathers and

a yellow beak. He is a parrot. Tommy lives in a cage with three other birds. At night he whistles

after he is fed.

6. Imagine you have to choose a classroom pet from a mouse, a bird, or a gold fish. List an **advantage** and a **disadvantage** for each of these classroom pets.

Choice	Advantage	Disadvantage
mouse		
bird		
gold fish		

From these advantages and disadvantages select four or more important things that a class should consider in selecting a class room pet.

_____

_____

_____

Consider one of these factors at a time. Give 3 points to the pet that you think is best for the factor, 2 points to the next best, and 1 point to the worst. Which pet has the most points?

Factor	Mouse	Bird	Gold fish
Total points			

7. One of the birds in each group is **different** from the others. Circle it and say why it is different. Make up your own group of birds with one different one. State the reason.

Groups	Reason
eagle sparrow pigeon	
emu magpie penguin	
duck pelican hawk	

8. List 2 ways of keeping a bird **outside** without using a cage.

_____

_____

9. Jack wants a parrot as a pet. His mother does not want a bird as a pet. Write down two **reasons for** and two **reasons against** Jack wanting a parrot as a pet.

Reasons for

_____

_____

Reasons against

_____

_____

10. Complete the statement:

If there were no more birds left in the world then _____

_____ and this would mean that _____

_____.

11. What kind of food (and where do you think it finds it) does a bird eat if:

a. it has a short strong beak?

_____

_____

b. it has webbed feet and a long beak?

_____

_____

c. has small claws and a long, thin, curved beak?

_____

_____

d. has long, curved claws and a curved, sharp beak?

_____

_____

Communications

Communication means the sharing of information. We can do this in many ways.

The most ancient form of communication, and one we share with other species, is 'body langauge' (use of the face and body to signal feelings and intentions). This is largely unconscious, instinctive communication.

Learned communication starts with listening and speaking – skills we pick up in early childhood. Later we learn to read and write. While speech is as old as human existence (perhaps 250,000 years), writing is a relatively recent invention, going back to the ancient Mesopotamians, and their cuneiform script, and to Egyptian hieroglyphics (about 3,000BC), as well as the much later Greek 'alphabet', or sound-sign system (about 800 BC), which has become the basis for all Western literature.

Printed Communication

The invention of writing led to books. Originally, only wealthy people could afford books, because they were copied by hand. However, the invention of mechanical printing using metal type letters (1455) led to mass produced books, and later to newspapers and magazines as well. Today, we have libraries full of books and literally thousands of magazines to choose from.

Photographic Communication

Photographs were used to record pictures back in 1826. It was another thirty-five years before coloured photos were possible. In the 1890s, movies were developed.

Electronic Communication

The telegraph, invented in the 1830s, allowed electric messages to be sent along wires. Then in 1876 the telephone allowed the human voice to be transmitted. About thirty years later, sounds were able to be sent through the air (radio). When television was invented (the 1920s), both pictures and sound could be transmitted to distant places. Today, satellite and internet links allow instant communication throughout the world.

Languages

Nearly 3000 languages are spoken around the world. English is one of the world's major languages.

Communications

1. Write down three ways in which a **newspaper** is the **same** as a **book**.

_____

_____

_____

Now write down three ways in which it **different** from a book.

_____

_____

_____

2. The following things have been placed in an **order**. What **property** of them was used to place them in this order?

letter   newspaper   book   encyclopaedia

Property used _____

3. Underline the one **fact** below.

a. Television is more interesting than radio.

b. Radio was invented before television.

c. You can learn better from a book than you can from TV.

d. Eventually there will be no need for newspapers.

Why is it a fact?

_____

_____

4. Mr Reader wondered why his newspaper was not in his driveway in the morning. He **assumed** that the paper delivery person was sick. What is Mr Reader assuming?

_____

_____

What do you think is the **reason**?

_____

_____

What **evidence** would you need to **prove** that you were correct?

_____

_____

5. Make a big list of **properties** or **features** of these media. Then cross out any properties **not common** to **all** of the media.

radio   newspapers   books   television

_____

_____

_____

Are there any properties that **all media** have in **common**?

All media _____

_____

6. Why do you think a newspaper has such **large** pages?

_____

_____

7. Why do you think many road signs use **black writing** on a **yellow background**?

_____

_____

8. Complete the following by placing **words** in the **blanks**.

If there were no more computers in the world then _____

_____ and this would mean that _____

_____ .

9. Write down a **reason for** and a **reason against** a person using the Internet.

Reason for

_____

_____

Reason against

_____

_____

10. Can you think of three places where you **could not** read a newspaper?

_____

_____

11. Make up two questions about **computers** starting with a word from row A and then one from row B. Try to answer your questions.

Row A	What Where When Which Who Why How
Row B	Is Did Can Would Will Might

eg Q. Who might not want to use computers?
    A. People who are frightened of new things.

Question 1

_____

_____

Answer

_____

Question 2

_____

_____

Answer

_____

Energy

Something has energy if it has the capacity to do work.

The Sun is the major supplier of energy to animals and plants on Earth. Humans also get energy from chemicals, electricity, machines, tides, wind, and nuclear-reactions.

Primitive people discovered millennia ago that wind, fire, and animals could be used as sources of energy to help them do work. Fire could be used to heat their caves or houses, and later to melt and create metals. Wind could be caught in sails to propel their boats. Animals could be harnessed and used to pull loads or lift weights.

Light energy is necessary for life on Earth. The green plants that make our oxygen need light to live. The light helps water and carbon dioxide to combine to form oxygen. This process is called photosynthesis.

Light from the Sun also heats the Earth so that it is habitable. Without the Sun's energy, there would likely be no life on this planet. Other things can give off light as well as the Sun. Early humans produced light from fires. Then they invented torches and other things that made light from electricity.

Heat energy is derived from burning fuels. This can be used directly – to cook food for instance – or used indirectly to create another product, such as electricity. Unfortunately, use of fuels creates a conservation problem. All of the Earth's deposits of oil, gas, and coal are being used up by humans at an alarming rate. They cannot be replaced. We will have to use more solar and nuclear power in the future.

Energy

1. Write down an example of **heat energy** as used in everyday life.

_____

_____

_____

Now write down an example of **light energy** as used in everyday life.

_____

_____

_____

2. Place the following things in an order. Say which **property** was used to place them in this order.

metal   heat   plough   fire

Your order _____

Property used _____

3. Write down one **advantage** and one **disadvantage** for using:
a. nuclear reactions
b. the wind
c. coal
d. the sun
to make electricity for use in homes.

	Advantage	Disadvantage
nuclear		
wind		
coal		
sun		

Now what are some **relevant factors** to consider about these methods in choosing one to make electricity for a state or country?

_____

_____

_____

43

4. Write in the missing **cause** or **effect** in the table below.

Cause	Effect
	thunder
sun on rain drops	
too much UV light	
too much friction	
electricity in thin wire	

5. Why do you think a **lens** in reading glasses:

a. has curved surfaces?

_____

_____

b. is made of glass?

_____

_____

6. Three things in each of the following lists are **different** in some way to the other three things. Circle them and say **why** they are different.

sunlight   wind   coal   natural gas   tides   oil

_____

_____

shadow   music   lens   explosion   ear   rays

_____

_____

force   temperature   insulation   weight   push   boil

_____

_____

copper   plastic   glass   iron   wood   steel

_____

_____

7. Write down five or so words that have something to do with **energy**. Add some words suggested by other people.

_____

_____

8. Write in a **key word** at the end of each row on the table below. Now write in 2 to 6 words as a **connector** to make a **sensible sentence**. Do this for another of your key words.

Topic	Connector	Key Word
eg Energy	is needed for us to do	work

Metals

The discovery of metals by humans allowed them to move out of the Stone Age. Iron was, and still is, a very important metal for humans.

It does not occur naturally, but is made by strongly heating carbon and iron oxide. In about 1000 BC, some people probably noticed that iron ore rocks around their camp fires formed a very strong, shiny metal in the coals. They learnt that this metal could be shaped into spear tips, knives and swords for killing animals and enemies.

Iron by itself is a brittle metal that snaps easily. In order to make it stronger, carbon and other metals are added to form steel. Steel is an example of an *alloy* or mixture of metals. Iron is one of the few metals used to make magnets. Nickel, like iron, is another metal that is magnetic or attracted to magnets. Scientists believe that the core inside the Earth is mainly molten iron and nickel.

Although only a few metals are magnetic, they all allow electricity and heat to pass through them. We say that they are 'conductors' or that they conduct electricity and heat. Some substances *look* shiny and hard like metals, but if they don't conduct electricity, they are probably non-metals or metal oxides.

The seventy or so different metals on earth are mainly found combined with oxygen as ores or oxides. These ores have to be mined from the ground. To make a pure metal, we have to remove the substances combined with the metal. Heating strongly with carbon or passing an electric current through the molten metal ore are common methods of making pure metals.

Metals such as gold, silver and platinum are rare, because they are found uncombined with other substances. These metals are very expensive. Consequently, they are generally used for making jewellery. Even 5000 years ago people used gold and silver for their jewellery.

Copper is another useful metal. However, it is soft and combines with water and air easily leading it to corrode to a green powder. Harder and stronger alloys of copper are made by adding metals such as tin or zinc to it. This forms alloys of bronze and brass.

Mercury is one of the few metals that is a liquid at room temperature. But, like all metals, it allows electricity to pass through it.

Different metals have different properties. For example, lead is very heavy, while aluminium is very light. Some metals, such as sodium, are so light that they float on water. Titanium is so strong that it is used in making parts of aeroplane wings and engines.

Metals

1. Write down five or so words that have something to do with **metals**. Add some words suggested by other people.

_____

_____

_____

2. Write in a **key word** at the end of each row on the table below. Now write in two to six words as a **connector** to make a **sensible sentence**. Do this for another of your key words.

Topic	Connector	Key Word
eg Metals	are good conductors of	electricity
Metals		
Metals		
Metals		

3. Now ask **why** or **how** of each sentence you have made. Write in your questions. Try to find an **answer** for each of your questions.

eg Q. WHY do metals conduct electricity?
    A. Electrons can pass through the atoms of metals.

Topic 1 _____

_____

Topic 2 _____

_____

Topic 3 _____

_____

4. Write down two ways in which **iron** is the **same** as **plastic**.

_____

_____

_____

Now write down two ways in which **iron** is **different** from **plastic**.

_____

_____

5. The following stages of making iron are **mixed up**. Put them in the order that they are **carried out in**.

purifying   crushing   mining   smelting

Correct order _____

6. Write down some **relevant** or **important properties** of metals that you think engineers considered when deciding on a metal to use in wires for carrying electricity in our homes.

_____

_____

7. Write down two **facts** about iron.

_____

_____

Now write down two **opinions** about iron.

_____

_____

8. Complete the following table. You may have to use a textbook to find the facts.

Metal	Magnetic	Shiny	Solid	Melts Easily	Conducts
copper	no	yes			
iron					
mercury					
gold					

Which **properties** are **common** to **all metals**? What **generalisation** can you make about metals?

_____

_____

9. You are a medieval inventor who wishes to construct a horseless carriage. Which of the metals listed in the table above would you use, and why?

_____

_____

48

10. Can you think of three **reasons** why:

a. coins are **round**?

_____

_____

_____

b. many coins are made of the metal called **nickel**?

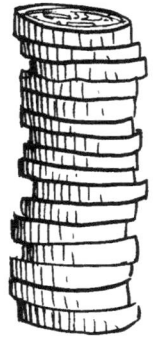

_____

_____

_____

11. Complete the following:

a. Iron is to solid   as   Nitrogen is to _____

b. Iron is to conductor   as   Wood is to _____

Pollution

Humans are polluting the sea, land and air every day. Factories pollute the air with smoke, poisonous gases and dust. Carbon dioxide from burning coal, oil and petroleum can pollute the air. Cars also poison the air as they move along, causing smog in big cities. This can make people's eyes itch and can even kill those who find it difficult to breathe. Pollution can stop heat from the sun escaping into space. If this happens the temperature of the air around the Earth can rise. Then the ice caps at the North and South Poles will melt, which will cause flooding. This effect is called the 'Greenhouse Effect'.

Factories pollute rivers with poisonous chemicals, which kills fish and animals that live in it. Oil tankers also pollute our oceans. Captains of tankers sometimes clean the oil out of their tanks while at sea. This oil can be washed up onto beaches and can kill birds and other sea creatures.

Every time we spray chemicals to kill insects or weeds we are poisoning the air. Farmers spray large amounts of insecticides and herbicides around their farms. Unfortunately, these kill birds as well as the insects eating the crops. Fertilisers added to soil to grow better crops also pollute water supplies. Rain washes these chemicals into rivers, which carry them into reservoirs that store our drinking water.

How can we help reduce the amount of pollution in the world?

Governments can pass laws, preventing people from polluting the air, water and earth. These laws can stop factory owners from piping poisonous chemicals into rivers or toxic gases into the air. They can control car emissions and use of farm chemicals.

Some people feel so strongly about factories polluting their air and water that they protest and expose such companies to the newspapers and television.

We must also educate people about the bad effects that pollution has on the quality of our lives. We can encourage them to save energy by using less electricity, using their cars less and recycling things such as glass, metal, paper and plastics.

We must also allow Nature to use its own cycles to destroy some of the pollution we make. For example, bacteria and oxygen can break down rotting animals and plants into nutrients or chemicals. These can then be used by living plants to grow bigger. These plants can be eaten by small creatures that can be eaten by larger creatures and so on.

Pollution is one of our biggest problems, and all concerned citizens should support moves to reduce it all over the world.

Pollution

1. Make up two questions about **pollution** starting with a word from row A and then one from row B.

Row A	What Where When Which Who Why How
Row B	Is Did Can Would Will Might

Try to answer your questions.

eg Q. Why is pollution bad?

    A. It poisons the air, sea, and land to kill the animals that live in them.

_____

_____

_____

2. Three of the following are **different** from the other three. Circle them and say why they are different.

air   noise   pesticides   water   smoke   soil

Different because all _____

_____

3. Write in two ways in which pollution of the **ocean** is the **same as** pollution of the **air**.

_____

_____

Write in two ways in which it is **different from** pollution of the air.

_____

_____

4. Write down four or more **causes of pollution** (pollutants). Can you see anything that is **common** to **all** types of pollution?

Pollutants _____

_____

_____

_____

Common features _____

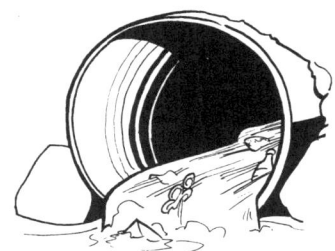

_____

_____

51

5. Some people like to kill flies with fly swats. Other people like to kill flies with fly spray insecticides. Write in an advantage and disadvantage of killing flies in your home by each method.

	advantage	disadvantage
fly spray		
fly swat		

6. Complete this statement:

If people continue to use freon gas to squirt mists of liquids from cans then _____

_____ and this could mean that _____

_____.

7. Fred sees many dead fish floating on top of the river in which he is fishing. List two things he can **definitely** be sure of.

_____

_____

List 2 things he **can't** be sure of without proof.

_____

_____

What do you think is the **reason** for the fish floating to the top of the river? What **evidence** would you need to **prove** you're right?

My reason _____

_____

_____

Evidence needed to prove it _____

_____

8. Underline the **fact** here.

a. There is more pollution today than there was 50 years ago.

b. There will be more pollution in 50 years time than there is now.

c. Young people care about pollution more than adults.

Why is it a fact?

_____

_____

_____

9. Underline the **cause** and circle the **effect** in the following.

a. There are laws to stop people from making too much noise.

b. Recycling allows us to use fewer new materials in making glass, metals, plastic, and so on.

c. The airplane flew low over the paddock. The pilot was very experienced. Insecticide was sprayed from the plane. That summer very little of the crop was attacked by insects.

Dinosaurs

Dinosaurs (from the Greek 'terrible lizards') weren't lizards, but they were cold blooded reptiles that lived on Earth 225 to 65 million years ago. Some were plant eaters, while others were flesh eaters. Some were up to 27 metres long and would have been able to look over a three story building. Some weighed 85 tons or 10 times the weight of an elephant. Others were less than a metre long.

The bones and footprints of dead animals were covered with mud millions of years ago. Under the pressure of layers of earth, these eventually turned to hard rock. Today scientists find very old bones, foot prints, and shells in this rock that help them to picture what life was like millions of years ago. These preserved bones and prints are called fossils. The dinosaurs lived on the Earth when it was warm and humid.

Some dinosaurs, like Tyrannosaurus Rex, were fast moving land dwellers, while others, like slow-moving Brontosaurus, spent most of the day in lakes.

Here are some properties of five of the most famous dinosaurs.

Dinosaurs	Laid eggs	Sharp teeth	Neck length	Meat eating	Number of legs	Small brain
Tyrannosaurus	yes	yes	short	yes	4	yes
Brontosaurus	yes	no	long	no	4	yes
Stegosaurus	yes	no	short	no	4	yes
Trachodon	yes	no	short	no	4	yes
Triceratops	yes	no	short	no	4	yes

54

Dinosaurs

1. Write down three ways in which a **dinosaur** is the **same** as an **elephant**.

_____

_____

_____

Now write down three ways in which it **different**.

_____

_____

_____

2. Underline the two **facts** here.

a. Dinosaurs were not warm blooded

b. Dinosaurs died out because smaller animals ate their eggs.

c. Someday scientists will breed dinosaurs in the laboratory.

d. Dinosaurs needed oxygen to live.

Why are they facts?

_____

_____

3. Mary concluded that dinosaurs died out because smaller animals learned to find their eggs and then they ate them. But what was Mary **assuming**? What else could have caused dinosaurs to become **extinct**?

_____

_____

4. Allosaurus was a dinosaur. From the table of facts about dinosaurs given with this topic what are four things you can be **sure of** about Allosaurus?

_____

_____

_____

5. Gila monster is a reptile in Mexico that lays eggs, has four legs, eats plants, and has a small brain. Is it a **dinosaur**? Why or why not?

_____

_____

6. Why do you think the Brontosaurus needed such a **long neck**?

_____

_____

_____

7. Why did dinosaurs, like other reptiles, **lay eggs** rather than have live babies?

_____

_____

_____

8. Name two types of animals that Tyrannosaurus **could not** catch and eat easily.

_____

_____

9. The answer is **dinosaur**. Make up two questions with this answer.

_____

_____

_____

10. Underline the **causes** and circle the **effect** in each of the following.

a. The Brontosaurus with its large body and small head ate quickly most of the day before it came from the lake.

b. The Brontosaurus ran into the lake as the Tyrannosaurus came over the hill.

11. From the table of facts about dinosaurs predict which type of dinosaur was the **last** to die on Earth? Say why.

Last to die _____

Reason _____

_____

12. The dinosaur Camptosaurus protected itself by running and hiding behind trees. What do you predict about its

a. Size? _____

b. Food? _____

c. Teeth? _____

13. The dinosaur Stegosaurus had soft teeth and it couldn't run quickly, it couldn't swim, and it couldn't hide easily. How do you think it **protected itself**?

_____

_____

_____

14. The dinosaur Anatosaurus had sharp teeth and webbed feet. What do you think it **ate**? Why?

_____

_____

_____

15. Complete the following with your own **ending**.

If there were dinosaurs in the world today then _____

_____and this would mean that _____

_____.

Food

Food gives us energy to move, grow, and keep healthy. Plants make their own food, but animals have to eat plants or other animals for their food supply. In some countries where there is not enough food, people spend most of their day looking for food in order to live.

Grains such as wheat, corn, and rice are used to make bread, cereals, cakes, and even alcoholic drinks. Vegetables and fruits come from the roots, flowers, and stems of plants. Meat comes from animals such as birds, fish, and land animals. Animals also supply us with eggs, fat, oils, milk, and other dairy products.

Sugars and starches, used in making such things as cakes, candy and bread, are called carbohydrates. With animal fats, they are the main source of fuel for our bodies to burn in order to keep us warm and to give us energy for movement.

Proteins found in eggs, nuts, fish, and milk are used to grow and repair any damage to our bodies.

Vitamins and minerals are also important things found in food. They are found in some meats, and a great many vegetables. It took many centuries for people to realise that without a 'balanced' diet (protein **and** cereals **and** vegetables), people could develop many diseases.

Vitamins and Minerals

Vitamin A	fights infection, keeps skin healthy
Vitamin B	good for muscles, growing, and nerves
Vitamin C	keeps blood vessels healthy
Iron	makes red blood cells
Calcium	for healthy bones and teeth

TRICKY THINKING PROBLEMS

Food

1. Write down three ways in which **sugar** is the **same** as **salt**.

_____

_____

_____

Now write down three ways in which it is **different** from salt.

_____

_____

_____

2. Complete the following.

Cheese is to milk   as   candy is to _____

Sugar is to plant   as   fat is to _____

Calcium is to teeth   as   iron is to _____

3. List three places where you **could not** eat food.

_____

_____

_____

4. The answer is **food**. List three questions with this answer.

_____

_____

_____

5. List three ways in which a pair of **socks** is the **same** as a **pizza.**

_____

_____

_____

6. Name four **different** uses for an **apple** other than to eat it.

_____

_____

_____

7. List three **interesting** ways of **encouraging** people to eat less food.

_____

_____

_____

8. Underline the **cause** and circle the **effect** in the following.

a. The fat person loved to eat many biscuits and cakes.

b. Oranges contain vitamin C which helps to keep colds away.

c. Milk comes from animals. It contains calcium. This is a mineral that helps to make strong bones.

9. Three of the following things to do with food are **different** from the other three. Circle them and say **why** they are different.

apples   biscuits   nuts   potatoes   bread   wine

Different because _____

_____

_____

60

Disasters

At 11.40 pm on 14 April 1912, the world's biggest passenger ship, The Titanic, struck an iceberg in the Atlantic Ocean. Although its builders had boasted that it was 'unsinkable', the giant ship rapidly filled with water. At 2.20 am, it broke in two and sank to the bottom of the sea. Less than 1,000 passengers had managed to climb into lifeboats and row away. In fact, there weren't enough lifeboats to go around, and more than 1,500 perished, trapped inside the hull, or killed by exposure in the icy water. It is arguably the most famous disaster of the twentieth century.

However, throughout human history, terrible events have claimed the lives of many innocents.

The legend of the lost civilisation of Atlantis is probably based on the destruction, nearly three millenia ago, of the island of Thera near Greece. Thera is a volcanic island. In 1470 BC, it blew up. The eruptions not only ended life on Thera, but sent terrible tidal waves which reached as far as Crete, 100 km to the south. Both islands were centres of the brilliant Minoan civilisation, which vanished, until rediscovered by modern archeologists.

Another historical disaster was the disappearance of Pompeii, in 79 AD. Pompeii was a seaside resort near Naples, in southern Italy. One hot summer, the nearby Mt Vesuvius erupted. Most inhabitants fled the city, but some were caught by the thick ash that fell or by the poisonous fumes from the mountain. As ash rained down, the city was quickly covered. Heavy rain followed, and the ash turned to stone. The area was abandoned, and finally forgotten. Under the ground however lay the perfectly preserved Roman city, most of its contents intact, together with some 2000 victims of the disaster. It is only in modern times that it has been excavated, and is now a major tourist attraction.

Perhaps the most terrible disaster of all was one that wiped out about a quarter of the total population of Europe, in the Middle Ages. It began with sailors bringing back a strange disease from Asia in 1347. The disease was marked by huge black swellings on the body. It spread rapidly. Most people who caught 'the Black Death', as it was called, died within days. People tried to escape it by dancing, or praying, or beating themselves for their sins. In fact it was spread by infected fleas, and the rats they lived on. During the next four years the plague killed some 25,000,000 people. Only when the fleas and rats died did the terrible tragedy come to an end.

Disasters

1. Write down something **common** to **all** disasters.

_____

_____

_____

2. The following disasters have been placed in an **order**. What **property** was used to place them in this order.

Titanic   Pompeii   The Black Death

Placed in order of _____

3. Give a **reason** as to **why** so many people died in the Black Death plague compared with Pompeii.

_____

_____

_____

4. Underline the two **facts** here.

a. The sinking of the Titanic was caused by stupidity.

b. The island of Thera was destroyed by a volcanic eruption.

c. The Black Death was the result of the wickedness of people in the Middle Ages.

d. Pompeii was lost for over a thousand years.

5. On Christmas Day, 1974, Cyclone 'Tracy' devastated Darwin, Australia, destroying the majority of buildings in the city and killing nearly 50 people. What could have been done to make this less of a disaster?

_____

_____

_____

6. In 1937, the German airship Hindenburg caught fire and crashed while landing at an airfield near New York. It was filled with hydrogen gas, which is lighter than air, and powered by four diesel engines on the outside of the ship. What can you predict was the **cause** of the disaster?

_____

_____

_____

62

7. Complete the following:

a. The Great Fire of London is to England as the San Francisco earthquake is to _____

b. Very strong winds is to cyclone as very heavy rains is to _____

c. Volcano is to Pompeii as _____ is to Black Death

8. The answer is **Plague**. Make up two questions with this answer.

_____

_____

9. Underline the **causes** and circle the **effect** in each of the following.

a. The San Francisco earthquake of 1906 saw falling buildings and fire, with massive loss of life and the destruction of 28,000 buildings.

b. The Great Fire of London occurred in the summer of 1666. Most buildings were made of wood closely built together, there was no fire brigade, and the winds were ferocious.

10. Here are a number of potential future disasters.

• An asteroid strikes Earth

• Global warming raises the sea level worldwide by 50 metres

• A new and deadly disease escapes from a laboratory

• The ozone layer in the Earth's atmosphere disappears

Choose one, and explain:

a. how it could happen

b. what effects it would have

c. who would be affected

d. what could be done (if anything) to prevent it occurring.

_____

_____

_____

_____

_____

_____

_____

Suggested Answers

Animals

1. Horse, cow, rabbit – because they are grass eating/non meat eaters.
2. Brain size.
3. He was assuming it was not dead by disease, old age, hit by something.
   Evidence needed: saliva in mouth, claw marks-blood, loose feathers.
4. Cat runs quicker, meows, climbs trees. Dog slower, barks, cannot climb trees.
5. So it can use two to hold food, defend itself, run faster.
6. All animals have head, eyes, body, mouth . . .
7. . . . is to bird, is to swim, is to bark.
8. Then more insects, more crops eaten by insects or less seeds dispersed by birds and this means that fewer plants/flowers/ crops.
9. For: safer to swim/surf, less people killed
   Against: sharks become extinct, food sharks eat will multiply rapidly in food chain.
10. Cats can't bark, talk, swim underwater, read . . .
11. Crab and fish both live in sea, swim, have mouth, lay eggs . . .
    Crabs only have shell, legs, claws, can live out of water.
12. On a truck weigh bridge.
13. Relevant factors: cost (buy and feed), size, noisy,can bring inside, colour, breed
    Irrelevant factors: time of day to buy it, shop or person to buy it from, who else has one
14. Who else saw it? How far from it? Did the observer use binoculars? Did he/she know what one looks like?

Insects

1. Butterfly only: has 4 wings, antennae, body segments, no blood vessels, 6 legs . . .
2. Facts are b and c. Evidence of b can be found in many examples; c can be seen by looking at fossils.
3. Generalisation: all insects have 6 legs, wings, can fly, are small, have antennae.
4. Some spare if damage frail legs, easier to hold on and to move in cramped spaces; stripes as camouflage in flowers.
5. . . . is to fruit, is to 8, is to antenna
6. If then flowers of fruit wouldn't be fertilised, meaning less fruit and vegetables.
7. For: so insects don't eat crop
   Against: pollute soil and air with poison insecticide
8. Both have antenna, make a noise, hard case . . .
9. No flies under water, in space, in insecticide factory/can
10. Mosquitoes, fleas, cockroaches, all harmful to humans.
11. Lay eggs, hatch maggots/larvae, form pupae/chrysalis.

Plants

1. Plants and animals both: are living organisms, have cells, need sun/water/air/food.
   Plants only: flowers, roots, branches, chlorophyll.
2. The sequence by which water passes through a plant.
3. Relevant: size, cost, drops leaves, activity of roots, poisonous
   Irrelevant: name, country where from, if other schools have them.
4. Roses are the prettiest. It's an opinion because 'prettiness' is an individual's judgement.
5. Sure: that some apples on ground, some on tree.
   Unsure: what caused apples to fall, what time they fell, if any will fall tomorrow.
6. All: trees here have leaves, a trunk, roots, branches

Exception: Palm trees . . . no branches, pine tree – no leaves.

7. Trees can't move to look for food. Leaves collect the small amount of carbon dioxide from air so need large numbers to get enough to grow.
8. . . . is to blood, is to oxygen.
9. Then less oxygen, more carbon dioxide, would mean atmosphere hotter.
10. For: more money for poor country/people
    Against: some trees extinct, less oxygen and more carbon dioxide in atmosphere.
11. Same because can sit in, take in/give off gases, many parts, different types, strong, can't talk/think.
12. No flowers at North Pole, in dark/under ground, inspace/vacuum, in a fire.
13. Wind/storm, sunlight/sap, leaves fall/change colour, bees attracted.

Whales

1. Both: live in sea, swim, tail, skin, eyes . . .
    Whales only: higher intelligence, blubber, warm blood, mammals.
2. Whales, cows, dogs . . . because all mammals: warm blood, suckle young.
3. Facts: whales are mammals, they migrate, very large.
    Opinions: they are nicer than sharks, no-one should kill them.
4. To take in large volumes of water containing small plankton; don't eat meat, filter off plankton to swallow.
5. . . . is to chicken, is to reptile, fat is to . . .
6. Then no whale watchers, would mean less tourism for some places.
7. For: basic food in diet of some people
    Against: becoming extinct.
8. Both move long distances, streamlined shape, make a noise . . .
9. Did anyone else see it? How far away was it? Have he/she ever seen one before? Did he/she use binoculars? Does he/she have good eyesight? Has he/she ever reported before?

Weather

1. Both: contain water, odd shapes, move in wind
    Clouds only: no shore, no tides, can't swim in, disappear.
2. Lightning, thunder, rain, flood – the order they occur in sequence.
3. Wind, tornado, breeze – all moving air.
4. 4b – both made of water.
5. Causes: sun on rain drops, lightning flash.
    Effect: no rain causes drought.
6. Disadvantages: spokes break, material tears, water comes in from sides.
    Changes: bigger covering, flexible spokes.
7. No air in space, in a vacuum, inside light globe, in a rock.
8. . . . air is to (made of), is to thunder (causes), barometer (measures).
9. Then we wouldn't know if/when/where going to rain/storm. This would mean that we might get wet without taking umbrella, more plane and boat accidents, people caught outside in storm.
10. Barometer, sun, water vapour, wind, tornadoes/gusts.

Planets

1. Both: round, heated by sun, solid, mountains, spin around sun.
    Earth only: water on it, air, planet, rivers, living things.
2. Distance of planet from sun.
3. Fact 3c: evidence from lunar landings proves it.
4. Round: gases or molten matter being thrown into shape as they spin rapidly

5. . . . is to star.
6. All planets: spin around sun, vary in size, average temperature less than 500 degrees, minimum year 88 days.
7. Then no more moon light meaning darker nights, no more tides meaning poor fishing.
8. What is the closest star? What allows life on Earth? What is the centre of our solar system?
9. Who else saw the comet? What size telescope was used? What is the experience of the astronomer? What is the reputation of the astronomer? Was he/she drunk or drugged?
10. Predict only: Jupiter 1000 days, - 200 degrees, 4 moons.
11. Moon not a planet, Sun is a star, Earth only one with life on it.

Birds

1. All birds are feathered (or winged), vertebrates with two legs, that lay eggs.
4. Food chain order: each being eaten by the next.
5. Relevant: black feathers,yellow beak, parrot.
6. Mouse – good: cheap to feed; bad: smelly,
   Bird – good: sings, active; bad: should be free,
   Fish – good: active; bad: can't hold
   Factors: cost to feed, easy of holding, activity, cleanliness.
7. Eagle: eats other birds, penguin-swims in sea or emu can't fly or magpie black and white, hawk-curved beak/eats mice.
8. Trimming wings, string on foot . . .
9. For: pretty, talks, active, view easily, leave for days with food
   Against: noisy, messy, costly to feed, can't handle easily, cruel to cage.
10. Then many more insects, means more plants eaten . . .
11. **a.** Short beak-seeds/nuts
    b. Fish/water animals -webbed feet for wading ,
    c. Nectar in flowers or insects in bark, beak to get into bark/flowers
    d. Meat/ animals, claws and beak for tearing flesh.

Communications

1. Both: on paper, index, title, authors, rectangular, printed
   Papers only: daily, many authors, current news, advertisements, few pages.
2. Order of amount of information / number of pages.
3. 3b.
4. Assuming that: no newspaper strike, no-one stole it, not under bush, not thrown next door. Evidence: evidence ring their home.
5. All media give information, edited by editors , journalists to write them.
6. Large pages easier to print, less folds, easier to see main page stories.
7. Road signs: most visible combination of colours.
8. Then more human jobs and calculations, would mean slower calculations, harder to store/transmit information, no internet.
9. For: latest information from around the world . . .
   Against: people spend too much time isolated in front of screen and not communicating live with friends.
10. Couldn't read paper underwater, in the dark, in country where don't know language of paper.

Energy

1. Fire – boiling water – steam – turbine – electricity.
   Light – photosynthesis – plant growth – animal growth – human food.

66

2. Fire – heat – metal – plough . . . order of fabrication.
3. Sun: free/clean, costly to make electricity, clouds!
   Wind: free/clean, costly to make electricity, no wind!
   Coal: doesn't depend on sunshine or wind, dirty/expensive/limited supply
   Nuclear: cheap/clean, risk of radiation
   Factors: cost, pollution, availability, cleanliness.
4. Lightning, rainbow, sunburn, heat, heat.
5. To refract (bend) light rays to focus on retina
   Transparent/easy to shape, easy to clean.
6. Coal, natural gas, oil: non-renewable sources
   Shadow, lens, rays: to do with light energy
   Force, weight, push: all forces
   Copper, iron, steel: all metals.

Metals

4. Both: solid, man made, moulded . . .
   Iron only: rusts, magnetic, conductor, made from ore.
5. Mining, crushing, smelting, purifying.
6. Relevant: cost, ease of drawing into wire, availability, resistance to electricity.
7. Fact: iron is an element, a conductor, magnetic, high melting point
   Opinions: iron is the most useful metal, iron should always be painted.
8. All metals conduct electricity.
9. Iron or copper: both workable but strong, and not too expensive.
10. Round because easy to make, store, handle, place in slots
    Nickel doesn't rust or wear easily.
11. . . . is to gas, is to non-conductor or insulator.

Pollution

2. Soil, water, air: things that can be polluted.
3. Both: involve chemicals, both move over surface of Earth
   Ocean pollution only: kills fish, harder to remove, involves oil.
4. Causes: oil, insecticides, smoke, poison – all chemicals.
5. Spray: quick/little effort/kills many flies, poisons air, stains surroundings, smells
   Swat: no cost/no pollution, messy, needs effort, can miss.
6. . . . then more freon (propellant) in air, so less ozone in atmosphere and more radiation
   to Earth, causing skin cancers.
7. Sure of: fish dead, fish bodies floating
   Unsure of: who did it, how done, when done, where done
   My reason: lack of oxygen due to algae in water
   Evidence: look for green algae on top of water.
8. 8a is a fact. We have evidence to prove it and also more people and pollutants.
9. Cause: laws   effect: reduces noise
   recycling   less new materials
   insecticide   little insect attack

Dinosaurs

1. Both: large, thick skin, four legs, plant eaters
   Dinosaurs only: layed eggs, extinct, many different kinds.
2. 2a and 2d.
3. Assuming meteorites, diseases, the ice age, etc did not kill dinosaurs.
4. Allosaurus laid eggs, 4 legs, small brain, extinct, blunt teeth.

5. Gila monster is not a dinosaur; not extinct/still alive now.
6. Long neck to reach leaves high in trees for eating.
7. Layed eggs because could hide eggs but not live born young from enemies.
8. Couldn't eat fish or birds as couldn't swim or fly.
9. Questions: is an extinct animal? what was Brontosaurus an example of?
10. Cause: large body/small mouth   effect: eat quickly
             Tyrannosaurus   ran into lake.
11. Tyrannosaurus as only meat eater so it ate other dinosaurs with its sharp teeth.
12. Camptosaurus: size, small, vegetation, blunt.
13. Stegosaurus: protected self with big spikes all over its body.
14. Anatosaurus: fish, sharp teeth means a meat eater, and webbed feet suggests it lived in lakes and oceans.
15. . . . then: they would have to be captured and kept in cages or reserves . . . and this would mean that people could study and look at them.

Food

1. Both: natural , crystalline, dissolve in water
   Sugar only: sweet, organic/from plants, made of molecules.
2. . . . is to sugar (made from), animal (source), blood (good for).
3. Couldn't eat: under water, upside down, in a mask.
4. Food: Sugar is an example of a . . . ? What is burnt by our bodies for energy? All animals need . . . to live?
5. Same: made by humans, smell, buy in a shop, keep you warm, different types.
6. Apple for: paper weight, pin cushion, a ball, cover a hole, decoration . . .
7. They halve everything they start to eat, are given money each day if they weigh less, they must drink two glasses of water before food . . .
8. Cause: love eating, effect: get fat
            vitamin C,   keeps colds away
            calcium   strong bones.
9. Bread, wine, biscuits not natural/made by humans.

Disasters

1. Many people involved, many deaths.
2. Property used is the number of people who died.
3. Reason: rats carried plague, rats can move over very large distances (compared to volcanoes/icebergs) to carry plague and plague lasts many years.
4. 4b and 4d.
5. Could have used stronger buildings and roofs (cyclone proof).
6. Hydrogen gas escaping from the interior of the ship was accidentally ignited, causing the whole airship to burst into flame.
7. . . . the USA, floods . . . , . . . rats/plague.
8. What caused the largest death toll in the Middle Ages? What is a disease carried by fleas which is mostly fatal to those who catch it? etc
9. Cause: earthquake   effect: loss of life, destruction of buildings
            wooden buildings, no brigade, winds   Great Fire of London
10. **Asteroid**: (a) accidental collision (b) tsunamis, dust cloud (c) potentially all people on Earth (depending on size) (d) rockets to deflect? **Global warning**: (a) greenhouse effect (b) flooding of coastal cities (c) millions of people (d) limit greenhouse emissions. **Disease**: (a) loose controls, terrorism (b)(c) millions of deaths (d) greater controls. **Ozone layer**: (a) pollution (b) solar radiation strikes Earth; skin cancer (c) everyone (d) greater controls.